Gideon's Principle

Stop Hiding From Who You Were Meant To Be!

Dustin J. Wilds

Printed in the United States of America

First Printing, 2021

ISBN 978-1-7379732-0-1

Follow Me on Facebook: Dustin Wilds, Author

Endorsements

An inspiring read for anyone battling with feelings of insignificance. The author becomes vulnerable while sharing his personal battle with such feelings that come from a lack of confidence. He provides insight into how the Biblical Character Gideon modeled a path to freedom from such traps that can limit any of us in our Holy Assignments.

Pastor Kelvin Page
Westmore Church of God
Cleveland, TN

Brother Dustin Wilds is among a group of men I deeply admire. He is genuine and preaches from the heart. His love of Christ shows in the pulpit as well as outside of the pulpit. Over the years, I have witnessed him show the love of Jesus to so many. His unconditional love for his family is unsurpassed. His passion for the church he pastors and leads shines brightly.

You will quickly see the qualities of the life Dustin lives every day. He is an encourager. This is so evident in this book. You will get a first-hand look at the journey Dustin took in the ministry and how it mirrors many of the same paths and directions Gideon took.

In this book, his transparency is truly on display especially in the chapter, "You Want Me to Do What?". He shares how God saw the potential in him and in each of us. It is up to us to accept the equipping and His calling.

I am convinced this book will encourage, challenge, and cause you to look for new ways to grow in your daily walk with Christ. As you will see, with God's anointing we can be overcomers and achievers.

I encourage you to read and reread this book many times. It will speak volumes to you, and you will find hidden nuggets each time you read it.

Richard Burnette
Sr. Vice President, Andrew Johnson Bank
Cleveland, TN

I am truly excited to recommend, "Gideon's Principle," to anyone who is seeking God's direction in their life! Dustin's ability to correlate his own experiences with those of Gideon helps this book speak directly to those of us who are searching for purpose and hope. As another pastor called to ministry in a less-than-traditional way, "God's ways are not our ways," really resonates. May we all take the challenges of this work to heart and surrender our imperfect vision to His perfect plan!

Rob Myers
Associate Pastor, First Baptist Church
Newport, Tennessee

In his book, Pastor Dustin Wilds gives us a very transparent look into his life and his journey to the calling of God on his life. Dustin reveals his struggles personally, in his marriage, in his calling, and in his acceptance into ministry, struggles that no matter what walk of life you are in, or come from, are very real to many of us. Dustin faces these battles with faith, and the strength and support of his wife and family and the Word of God. In his journey, he rises above unbelief, fear, and anxiety to become a mighty man of valor for his family and the kingdom of God.

Dustin places himself in the shoes of Gideon and allows Gideon's journey to mold him and encourage him to become who God always knew he could be. His insight to this is written in the pages of this book and used to remind us that regardless of how ill-equipped we seem to be, we were always perfectly equipped to do His will, regardless of the challenge or obstacles before us. Because God is with us and makes nothing impossible for us. I recommend this book to everyone who is battling feelings of unworthiness, anxiety, and fear of stepping out to be what God has called them to do. After all there is a little Gideon inside us all!

Glen Key
Pastor, Lone Oak Church of God
Signal Mountain, TN

Wonderfully written book that gives insight into how God operates when calling His children to action. Both long-time followers of Christ and new believers will gain useful knowledge from Gideon's calling while also learning from Pastor Wilds' personal experience with Gideon's Principle.

H.G. Sims, III, MD

Thank You

There are so many people who have encouraged me along this journey, that I am afraid I would leave someone out if I listed names, but you know who you are, and I thank you for your support.

The congregation of Lakeview Community Church; your commitment to the growth of the kingdom is unparalleled. Thank you for your unwavering commitment as we pursue the vision that God has laid before us.

To my mom and Dad, thank you for raising Dennis and I with the belief that, with hard work and the right attitude, we could accomplish anything, and for providing the atmosphere for us to be successful.

A Special Thank You

Renee Lynn - for reading, rereading, and then reading it again and correcting all of my grammatical errors. Who knew that those little commas, semicolons, and hyphens could make such a big difference!

Suzanne Burns - for guiding me through this process. Not only have you given of your time, but you have encouraged me not to quit when I wanted to give up, and you helped me to believe that I was an author, and I had a story to tell.

Dedication

I would like to dedicate this book to my wife Letisha, and our three kids, Elijah, Emma, and Ethan.

First off to Letisha, I could fill this book with words expressing what you mean to me, but I will just simply say thank you! You have always been my biggest fan and encourager. You are also a fierce protector. None of this would be possible without you. I don't even know if I would be here if God hadn't brought us together when He did. You are always pushing me to chase my dreams and not settle for mediocrity. You are the glue of our family. I love you and can't wait to see how many more dreams we chase down together.

To Elijah, Emma, and Ethan, don't ever doubt that you all are the greatest blessings that your mom and I have. It is a joy to watch you all grow up and mature into the young men and woman, that God is calling you to be. Your mom and I are very proud of you. Don't ever settle and don't ever let anyone else determine what you can and can't accomplish. You all are destined for great things. I love you all very much.

Gideon's Principle
Becoming Who You Were Meant To Be

Table of Contents

Introduction

Do you often find yourself on the sideline when you desperately want to get into the game?

Do you feel like you constantly watch others get that promotion, start their own business, go back to school, or change careers so they can spend more time with their families?

Are you the one that secretly wishes you had the courage other people do, but instead of taking that chance your fears keep you on the sidelines of life?

If this is your attitude, then you probably find that it surfaces in most, if not all, areas of your life, from your job to how you compare yourself to others.

You probably think you have some good ideas for your children's PTA group, but fear of what the other parents might think keeps you silent.

You may have a desire to coach your kids' sports team – but little Jimmy's dad played college ball, so you're probably not qualified enough.

Maybe you would like to teach a Sunday School class, lead a small group, or get involved in some other ministry at church, but there is always that thought that you can't shake.

The one that says you're not good enough, you haven't been saved long enough, you will fail, or surely God won't use someone like you.

Doesn't He know about your past?

Well guess what?

God is not concerned with your past, only your future.

By the way, you are not even close to being the only person that is held back by their fears. Many people go through life never coming close to achieving what God has for them because of fear.

When I tell you I understand, it's coming from someone who has dealt with fear, anxiety, and severe panic attacks off and on throughout most of my adult life.

Many times, the fear and anxiety would keep me from functioning on a normal, healthy level.

I couldn't go to work. I lost weight at a rapid pace because I couldn't eat. And I couldn't even begin to describe to you what a good night's sleep was like.

Even though I have a terrific wife and she never wavered from my side through it all, the anxiety and fear that I was experiencing took a toll on our marriage. Instead of me being the strong one, that fell on her.

It kept me from being the leader and the provider, and the protector of my family.

It constantly occupied my thoughts and kept all my attention on myself – not where it should have been.

You know what I finally realized?

This was exactly what the enemy wanted.

I was following the enemy's plan for my life instead of God's.

The enemy had me isolating myself and not only was I fearful and anxious, but depression wasn't far behind. I was so ashamed and embarrassed that I didn't want to ask for help and didn't know who to ask if I wanted too.

Guess what?

God has a plan for me, and He has a plan for you too.

His plan doesn't include fear, anxiety, and depression; matter of fact, His word tells us that He hasn't given us the spirit of fear (2 Timothy 1:7), and also that no weapon formed against us will prosper (Isaiah 54:17).

He also tells us throughout His word many, many times "Do not fear" or "be not afraid". In fact, He says it over 365 times! One for every day of the year!

You probably just said to yourself, this is easier said than done.

You are 100% correct, it won't be easy. But if I can do it, so can you.

Let me show you how far God has brought me.

On my lowest day, when I was around 30 years old, I came in from work and curled up in my wife's lap and cried like a baby. I didn't know what was wrong with me.

The anxiety had such a stronghold on me it was causing obsessive compulsive behaviors. I would constantly check my pulse and if I wasn't checking my pulse, then I was checking my blood pressure.

What this did was create a vicious never-ending cycle. Because of my anxiety I would check my blood pressure and heart rate.

Well, of course because of the anxiety, both of them would be elevated, which would cause me to panic and make my anxiety even worse.

Talk about a vicious cycle!

Finally, I went to the doctor and told him I thought I was going crazy, but crazy or not I was determined to make a stand.

I told the doctor if something is physically wrong with me, you fix it, that's your job, but if it's not physical, then tell me. And I'll fight it.

The doctor looked at me and said, Dustin, I don't think it's physical. I told him right then to get me off of all the medicine, that I knew what I needed to do.

I turned it over to the Lord. I began to focus my prayers on my anxiety. Then to reinforce it, I began to fast in companion with my prayers.

Not long after, I began to realize how the enemy was using the anxiety to hinder and cripple me. The anxiety was a physical manifestation of a spiritual battle that was taking place inside me.

Did I enjoy going through this?

No way, but what I came to realize was that the Lord was teaching me how the enemy was coming against me. Scripture says that we should not be ignorant of the enemy's devices (2 Corinthians 2:11).

One of the main keys for us to be successful in battle is to realize how the enemy works. Something that we need to understand about the enemy is he doesn't attack each of us the same way.

You want to talk about something that was hard to realize?

Think about the fact that God allowed me to suffer and go through this to make me stronger and position me for success.

Today I have learned how to recognize the anxiety and fear when it starts to come at me. Now, instead of waiting on it to attack me, I have learned to hit it head on.

When I realized this, at 32 years old, God changed my career.

I was a supervisor for one of the largest trucking companies in America. In 2006, without going to seminary and with very little training, God opened a door and called me into full time ministry.

Then at 36 years old, just three years later, He opened the door for me to pastor my first church. Now 12 years later, I am still serving as the pastor of that church.

Not only has it grown from 20-something members to over 200, but we have seen God do some pretty amazing things.

I have stepped into the role as the spiritual leader of my house and my marriage is stronger than ever.

My wife and I have three wonderful teenagers who are our greatest blessings in life.

Can I tell you that I never have to deal with anxiety and fear anymore? No, I can't.

From time to time, it still rears its ugly head and tries to get me to throw in the towel. But instead of quitting, I have learned to dig in deeper and let God use it to strengthen me.

I want to encourage you today. Know that you too can overcome the anxiety and fear that holds you prisoner.

Throughout the pages of this book, I will share with you my story and how God has worked in my life.

Together we will learn the Gideon Principle – Becoming Who You Were Meant to Be!

Blessings,

Pastor Dustin Wilds
Lakeview Church of God
Cleveland, TN

Chapter 1

Journey of a Lifetime

This book, "Gideon's Principle", is very personal to me.

Not only does it contain Biblical principles that I think anyone can apply to their lives and become the person that God has planned for them to be, but it contains some of my most personal experiences that I have been through on my way to becoming who God has called me to be.

I share with you some of my biggest victories, as well as some of my greatest moments of despair.

I share these moments not to draw attention to myself or to say look at me, but to show how God walks with us and works in us every moment of every day in every situation.

My desire is not only to lift up God and give Him the credit that He so rightly deserves, but to encourage everyone who reads the pages of this book and applies these principles to their life, to understand that God will do for you what He did for me.

Where do I begin?

I was 26 years old, newly married to a beautiful girl named Letisha, and had a great job making decent money.

You would think everything was great.

From the outside you would have thought we were living the dream. Let me tell you what you couldn't see.

Even though I was 26, I was not ready for marriage. I was a very selfish and immature individual.

The early years of our marriage were full of tension and many arguments.

There was no peace in our home, our relationship was not healthy at all. We both wondered how long it would last.

When it came to my job, I was employed by a large trucking company, making good money for someone my age, but to be honest we were broke.

I couldn't even pay the bills.

You see, I brought something into our marriage that Letisha knew nothing about.

I had a major addiction to gambling.

I am not talking about a few dollars here and there or I bought a lottery ticket on Fridays.

I am talking about getting paid on payday and not coming home until I was broke.

I am talking about having your furniture repossessed because you couldn't make the payment.

I am talking about lying to my wife and staying gone for days chasing this crazy addiction.

The problem was I couldn't see that I had a problem.

It makes no sense at all, looking back.

My family was telling me that I needed help, my marriage was a wreck, my behaviors were not normal. But I couldn't see it.

Or should I say I didn't want to see it.

My addiction with gambling started early. In grade school we would pitch quarters against the wall and the winner got all the quarters.

Then in high school we graduated to playing blackjack during homeroom and running parlay sheets during football season.

When I started working, it wasn't unusual for me to put a big portion of my paycheck in the poker machine at the back of the convenience store where I worked.

After I graduated and moved into the workforce, I started to place bets with the local bookie. As you can imagine as I made more money, the bets became larger.

My hang-up was not betting on the ball games. That didn't really excite me too much.

What got me hooked was playing cards.

I wanted to know that I was better than the person sitting across from me.

I was so hooked that when I went broke with my own money, I would borrow money to gamble with.

It was so bad that when I finally quit gambling, it took me five years to pay off all of my debts or should I say us.

Because at this point it wasn't just me, but it was affecting Letisha also.

I couldn't see that I had a problem because the addiction happened so gradual and over a period of time. When I got married, I even quit gambling for a while.

This reinforced my belief that I didn't have a problem.

My attitude was, "See? I can quit whenever I want to."

Then the bottom fell out.

One night my neighbor called and asked if I wanted to get together with him and some of the guys and play quarter poker.

What was the harm? It was just quarters.

The addiction came back with a vengeance.

The very next night, I was back playing in the big games for thousands of dollars. As you would expect, this had a major impact on my marriage in a negative way.

I can't tell you how many of our nights ended in screaming arguments because I had lied to Letisha and went and gambled.

I remember one particular night, as I was pulling in the driveway about two or three o'clock in the morning, Letisha was coming out the front door with an armload of my clothes, throwing them out in the yard.

I knew there wasn't much use in saying anything.

I knew that she would stay mad at me for a few days, so I just picked up enough clothes to do me for two or three days and left.

My grandmother was out of town, so I went to her house and stayed. I was so messed up that instead of seeing the dire situation of my marriage, I thought, "now I can go gamble for a few days without having anyone to answer to."

You may wonder why I would share such a personal story with you.

It was definitely not one of my best moments.

Yes, to be honest, looking back I am embarrassed and ashamed of my actions.

But I share it because that may be a chapter in my story, but it is not how my story ends.

I want you to understand that no matter what you have done or where you are at right now, your situation can change.

This is not what God has planned for you.

But you have to learn to turn the page.

My turnaround started one night when our situation finally came to a head. It was the same as usual, I had lied to Letisha and took off to do my thing.

I never would tell Letisha where I was going, but I would always let my neighbor know in case anything happened. That way he knew where to get a hold of me, in an emergency.

This night Letisha had had enough.

She was over it. She called my neighbor and asked him where I was. She told him that she was through. She was going to come and get me, but then it was over.

She couldn't go down this road anymore. My neighbor told her that he wasn't going to tell her where I was because nothing good would come from it if she showed up where I was.

He went on to tell her not to make a drastic decision.

He told her, yes Dustin has a problem but one thing I know is that he loves you. You don't see it and he doesn't always act like it, but he loves you.

A few hours later I came in broke and expecting the worst. I expected us to fuss like every other night, but this night was different.

There was no screaming or arguing.

As we sat on the edge of the bed, I looked at Letisha and told her that I wanted her to divorce me. I told her that she deserved better. That she deserved someone that would take care of her and provide for her and that I wasn't that guy. That I didn't know how to be a good husband.

Then I said the words that forever changed my life.

I said, "You find someone that will take care of you and let God do with me what He will."

I, of course, thought God would kill me, but instead He had other plans.

Letisha walked over to me that night and put her arms around me and said, I am not going anywhere.

She went on to tell me that she didn't know how we would make it, but we were going to make it.

I didn't realize it at the time, but when I said those words, I had just given God permission to have His way in my life.

That night we started a journey that we are still on today. We started the journey of discovering who God meant for us to be and figuring out the plan that He has laid before us.

Can I tell you that I don't make any more mistakes and that Letisha and I always get it right?

No, absolutely not, but what I can tell you is that we are a whole lot better than we used to be.

We have come to understand that God's plan for us is so much better than what we could have ever imagined.

I invite you now as you read this book to start your own journey with the Lord.

Apply the Gideon Principle to your life and become the person that God has always meant for you to be.

Chapter 2

The Gideon Principle

What is the Gideon principle?

What I call the Gideon principle is where God takes someone that is so unassuming and that not too many people think would accomplish much, and He uses them to achieve great things.

We all like a good underdog story and the Bible is full of them. I guess probably the most famous one and the one that most people think of first is the story of David and Goliath.

When it comes to heroes in the Bible, I like to think of myself like David.

He is a man of tremendous courage and in the face of danger he shows no fear.

When he hears of Goliath coming against the armies of Israel, he fearlessly and courageously proclaims to king Saul, "Let no man's heart fail because of Goliath; thy servant will go and fight with this Philistine." (1 Samuel 17:32)

Here David is just a shepherd boy, he's not militarily trained or even fought in his first battle with the army, yet without hesitation he is willing to do what even the greatest warriors of Israel are afraid to do.

When Saul objects, David gives the reasoning that when he was watching his father's sheep a lion and a bear came to take some and David pursued both the lion and the bear, slew them, and rescued the sheep (1 Samuel 17:32 - 36).

David realized that the battles he faced today that God had prepared him to fight them in the past. Not only had God prepared him to fight them, but God had prepared him to be victorious.

God will not lead you into any battle that He has not prepared you to win. David goes out and slays Goliath and becomes a national hero in Israel.

I can't prove it, but in my mind, I believe that it was in that valley, as David stood facing Goliath, that part of the words to the 23rd Psalm came to him, "Yea though I walk through the valley of the shadow of death, I will fear no evil for Thou art with me; Thy rod and Thy staff they comfort me" (Psalm 23:4).

The story of David and Goliath is truly one of the great underdog stories, but what if I told you of one where the odds of failure were even greater?

I don't want to put down or diminish David in any way.

He truly was a man after God's own heart.

But when it came to him facing Goliath, it was one on one.

Yes, it was giant against teenager.

It was warrior against shepherd.

It was sword and spear against slingshot and stone, but it was still just one on one.

No matter how big Goliath appeared, David still had to just defeat one person.

When it comes to the story of Gideon, he led 300 men against an army of 135,000 Midianites.

For each ONE soldier in Gideon's army of 300, there were 450 in the Midianite army.

You want to talk about seemingly impossible odds.

One thing that we know, no matter how many in the enemy army, with God on our side, we are never outnumbered.

Just like David, won a great victory for Israel, so did Gideon. Gideon's victory is one of the greatest military victories that the world has ever seen.

In both cases, we know that David didn't defeat Goliath on his own and Gideon's 300 didn't defeat the Midianite army on their own.

David and Gideon realized that their successes depended on God working and fighting on their behalf.

This is the heart of the Gideon principle!

When we realize that we are nothing on our own, and when we put our faith in God, even the least of the least can overcome the greatest odds and be successful.

The Bible tells us in 1 Corinthians 1:27, "But God hath chosen the foolish things of the world to confound the wise; and God hath chosen the weak things of the world to confound the things which are mighty".

Usually at first, we might find it offensive to be associated with this verse. Who out there likes to be called foolish or weak?

Over the years, I have learned to embrace this verse and I even tell people God wrote this verse about me.

Now, not only does this verse not offend me, but I love the fact that I can relate so personally to a scripture that gives us insight on how God operates.

Why do I say that?

Because the way my life unfolded, I would have never thought that I would end up in the ministry, pastoring a church that is growing and making a difference in the community around us for God.

I remember one time after I had become a pastor and my wife and I had moved to Cleveland, we went to my parents for a few days.

While we were there, I got an opportunity to spend some time with my mom and dad's neighbor.

He was an elderly gentleman that had seen me grow up through my middle school and high school years into adulthood.

I wasn't a mean kid, but I always didn't make the right choices and we will just leave that there.

This neighbor had pretty much seen all the highs and lows that I went through growing up.

I remember in our conversation, that he told me how proud he was of the way that I turned out.

We called him Rip, and I said to him, "Rip, in a million years, I never thought that I would have turned out to be a pastor.

I'll never forget his response. He laughed a big old belly laugh, and said, "Dustin, that makes two of us."

Even though I didn't realize it at the time, his response envelops the idea and the concept of the Gideon principle.

In the human society, everything has to make sense in order to work or be explained. In math, everything has a formula or a quotient behind it to explain it.

In science there are certain laws or theories that everything must fall under.

But when it comes to how God operates, when it comes to the Gideon anointing, there are no rules which govern how things turn out.

There are no laws that serve as guides to explain things.

Why is this?

Because God is not bound by human limits.

He tells us in Isaiah 55:8 and 9, "For My thoughts are not your thoughts, neither are your ways My ways, saith the Lord. For as the heavens are higher than the earth, so are My ways higher than your ways, and My thoughts than your thoughts".

To humans, it doesn't make sense that David defeated Goliath.

It doesn't make sense that Gideon's 300 defeated 135,000.

And to Rip and I, it didn't make sense that I was a pastor.

The beauty of the Gideon principle is that when we operate in faith, it elevates us above the limits of man's formulas and laws and moves us into the realm of God's possibilities.

In twelve years of pastoring, I have been involved in and seen things that I can't explain.

I have laid hands on and prayed for a lady with failing kidneys only to receive a testimony of how they were showing tremendous improvement at her next doctor's appointment.

I have prayed with a man that had sores on his body that wouldn't dry up.

According to his testimony, they began to dry up the instant we prayed.

When medicine wasn't doing its job, I have seen fevers break and blood pressure return to normal in response to a prayer.

I have seen people that were substance dependent for twenty years delivered in an instance. I have seen alcoholics come into a service drunk and leave sober.

I have seen relationships reconciled when almost no one gave them any hope.

I have seen cancers cured, babies healed, addicts delivered, and relationships restored in ways that just didn't make any human sense.

It didn't make sense to David's family that he was chosen king, but God had a plan.

It didn't make sense to Gideon that God chose him, but God had a plan.

It didn't make sense to my neighbor that I was a pastor, but God has a plan.

What you feel inside about yourself might not make sense to you or anyone else, but God has a plan.

Let's discover that plan and learn how to embrace the Gideon principle.

Chapter 3

From Wimps to Warriors

Well as much as I would like to imagine myself as the bear chasing, lion taming, giant slaying, no fear, full of courage, hero of Israel, I am probably more like Gideon than I am David.

Many times, in life, I have given into my own fears before the battle ever started.

I have often thought of myself as underqualified, overlooked, and inexperienced.

Why would anyone choose me?

How is there any way that God can use me to accomplish anything at all, let alone anything great?

This is very much the same way that Gideon thought of himself.

He saw himself as the least of the least, unworthy, and unable to do anything great.

My connection with Gideon started on October 14, 2001, at the Newport Church of God in Newport, Tennessee.

Our nation had just come under attack the month before on September 11 with the planes flying into the twin towers and also the Pentagon.

For my wife, Letisha, who grew up a preacher's kid, and was running from God, this was a call to reconcile her relationship with the Lord.

For me, I knew enough about the Bible to just cause myself confusion and think this was about to be the end of the world. It caused me a great deal of fear and anxiety because I knew I wasn't ready to meet the Lord.

Anyways, misguided or not, we found ourselves in church the very next Sunday and the journey began.

My wife Letisha responded immediately.

That first Sunday she knew what she had to do, and she made things right with the Lord.

With me it took slightly longer, but a few weeks later, on Sunday night October 14, it happened.

We came to church and literally sat in the very back row.

The church was Pentecostal, and everything was relatively new to me. I didn't know much about Pentecostalism and knew very few people in the church.

To be honest, I really wasn't sure if I was comfortable being there or not, but that night my life forever changed.

I didn't know it at the time, but God had a divine appointment set up for me.

The Pastor, Bishop Charles Oaks, who later became a great friend and mentor, preached a sermon entitled, "Turning Wimps into Warriors".

It was the story of Gideon.

When the sermon was over, and the altar call was given a battle began to take place inside of me.

My heart was racing, my hands were sweating, and I had a death grip on the back of the pew in front of me.

My heart kept telling me to go to the altar and give it all to God, but my mind was telling me that you don't know any of these people and you will just embarrass yourself.

All I wanted to do was go up there and tell Pastor Oaks that I wanted to be a warrior for God.

I reasoned in my mind that if he had everyone close their eyes and bow their heads that I would run up there and tell him just that and then return to my seat before anyone saw me.

Well, guess what, as I have learned many times in ministry God has His own way of doing things and they are not necessarily the way that I want to do them.

Pastor Oaks stopped the service and in front of everyone, he called me out. Man, you talk about being scared and nervous.

He looked at me and said, "Son, you on the back row, I don't even know your name, come here".

I got out of my seat and walked towards the altar.

I felt like it took forever to get there, but Letisha said it was just like I was flying up the aisle. When I got there, he didn't say anything, instead he just looked at me like I was supposed to say something.

Well, this was all new to me. I didn't know what to do, but I knew that I wanted to say one thing. I looked up at him and said, "I want to be a warrior for Christ".

When I said that, I can hardly describe all the feelings that rushed through my body.

It was like I was stronger than I had ever been in my life, and at the same time, the greatest weight I had ever carried was taken away from me.

To this day, I still want to be a warrior for Christ.

I want to serve God as hard as I ever enjoyed the world. And I want to make a difference in the lives of others.

Can God really do with me what He did with Gideon?

The answer is yes, and He will do it with you too, if you will let Him.

Chapter 4

Who Am I?

Before we ever walk in the anointing or accomplish what God has called us to do, we must realize who we are.

Let me just go ahead and make this announcement:

Who we think we are and who God says we are, are usually worlds apart.

Look with me in Judges chapter 6, where we see God send an angel to commission Gideon for service.

Gideon is hiding in the winepress doing his work, when all of a sudden, an angel of the Lord appears to him and calls him a mighty man of valor.

Gideon immediately says to the angel, you've got the wrong guy. You have gotten me mixed up with someone else. (Paraphrasing of course)

Can you imagine an angel showing up to give you a message from the Lord and you telling him that he has made a mistake?

That is exactly what Gideon does.

Gideon tells him that not only is he from the weakest clan, but he is the weakest in the clan. Gideon describes himself as the weakest of the weak.

I want you to notice something right here.

From this first time that God spoke to Gideon, He refers to him as a mighty man of valor.

God never refers to Gideon as a wimp or as the least in his clan. When we see those terms, it is always Gideon referring to himself that way.

Gideon's own impression of himself has him set up for failure. Gideon is not the only one guilty of this, we often do this to ourselves, too.

We tend to view ourselves in comparison to other people around us. We form an opinion of ourselves based on whether we are as successful as those we look to.

My daughter, Emma, when she was in the 3rd, or 4th grade played on the school basketball team.

Bless her heart, she was so little that she could barely get the ball up to the goal.

She would get pushed and knocked around because she wasn't as big as some of the other girls.

One game she even got her nose busted. She came to her mother and I and wanted to quit but we wouldn't let her.

We told her that she didn't have to play the next year if she didn't want to, but she had to finish this year, because she had made a commitment to her team.

It was disappointing to us because even though she was so little, she showed some potential.

Her coach was great with her and recognized that she had some fear in her because of what had happened.

He made her a deal and told her that if she would play one quarter and give it everything she had, then the rest of the game she could help him coach.

She loved it.

She would play her quarter and then she would help the coach make decisions for the rest of the game.

She didn't realize it, but she was developing her Gideon anointing by learning to face her fears and overcome them.

Just the way God works things out, at the end of the season when the team voted for their all-star picks, Emma's own teammates voted her onto the all-star team.

She never played basketball again, but God used that experience to mold and shape her.

God never compares us to anyone. He sees us as the person we can be or will be.

He always looks at us as He intends us to be and then works to help us realize who we can be.

God always knew Emma could be an all-star, but He had to take her through the process to get her to realize it.

How we view ourselves has a tremendous impact on what we accomplish in life. All of Gideon's life, he probably had been picked on and made fun of for being weak.

This had happened so much that Gideon just accepted that that was who he was. He began to see himself the way others saw him.

So many of us are guilty of this, we let other people determine who we are and who we can become.

I know firsthand that if I had listened to other people, I would not be a pastor right now or I would have quit long ago. I would run into people from my past from time to time and they would ask what I was doing now.

The response was almost always the same, they would laugh and not believe me when I would tell them that I was pastoring a church and living for the Lord.

Not only did people from my past doubt my new identity but so did some of my new colleagues in the ministry.

When I first became a pastor there was a minister that came by and attended one of our services. After service, as we were talking, he asked me how I got to pastor a church in Cleveland, TN. (Cleveland is the headquarters of our denomination, and a lot of ministers want to pastor here.)

Before I could even answer he followed up with the question, who do you know?

When I finally did get to answer him, my answer was very simple.

Who do I know? I know the Lord.

I don't know what happened to that guy, but he was looking for his success to come from others.

He was looking for his promotion and placement to come from man.

The only person I could depend on was the Lord.

When the Lord is the only person, you can depend on for success, you better believe it's going to be greater than you could have ever imagined.

My attitude has always been that if the Lord wants me in a certain position or place, then He knows the best way to get me there.

When it comes to the Lord, He has a habit of using those that are underestimated, underappreciated, undervalued and overlooked.

A lot of times, God's choices don't make sense to us.

He picked Abraham, who was the son of a heathen idol maker to become the father of His nation. (Genesis 12:1-3)

He picked Moses who argued with Him that he wasn't qualified because of his stuttering to go before Pharaoh and lead Israel out of captivity. (Exodus 4:10)

He took Jacob, who was a liar and a thief and turned him into the nation of Israel. (Genesis 32:22-32)

He took David, a lowly shepherd and turned him into one of the greatest kings. (1 Samuel 16:1-13)

He used Rahab the harlot to save the Jewish spies and then later she is known as grandmother to Jesus, Himself. (Joshua 2:1-15)

He took twelve fishermen, businessmen, and tax collectors and used them to change the world as they became Jesus' disciples. (Mark 3:13-19)

If God can take all these people and do what He did with them, and He can take Gideon, a wimp by the world's standard and make him a mighty warrior, what can he do with you and me?

If I was going to be a successful pastor, then I had a choice to make.

I could either accept who the world saw me as, or I could choose to believe what God said about me.

He said that all things were possible through Christ Jesus. (Matthew 19:26)

He said that I was the head and not the tail. (Deuteronomy 28:13)

He said that I was an overcomer (1 John 4:4), and more than a conqueror (Romans 8:37). He said that I was a victor and not a victim (1 Corinthians 15:57).

Believe it or not, God didn't just say these things about me, He said them about you too.

Every day we have a choice to make.

We can believe what others say about us, think about us and expect of us, or we can choose to believe the One that created us, the One who knows every single detail about us.

Who knows more of what we are capable of, the One who created us and gave us our talents and abilities, or everyone else that when it comes to knowing us has barely scratched the surface?

The answer is easy, of course Jehovah our Creator knows everything about us.

The Bible tells us that He knows the number of hairs on our head, or in some cases, the lack thereof (Luke 12:7)!

The question is, who are we going to get our identity from?

Gideon chose to believe the Lord.

I choose to believe the Lord.

Who will you choose to believe?

Chapter 5

You Want Me To Do What?

God told Gideon that He was going to use Gideon to defeat a great Midianite army and deliver Israel.

This seemed impossible to Gideon, and he went straight into questioning God and making excuses.

I can almost see Gideon with wide eyes and a squeaky voice saying, "You want me to do what? God, You must have the wrong guy."

I know that is how I felt when I received my first ministry assignment.

I had been saved for a few months.

Everything was new to me, but I was like a sponge trying to soak up everything I could.

Pastor Oaks came to me one Sunday after service and said he had something he wanted me to do. He told me he wanted me to be an assistant in our 11-12-year-old Wednesday night boys' class.

I was like Gideon. I was terrified.

You are probably thinking, you are only going to be an assistant and it's just 11- and 12-year-old boys.

First of all, I didn't think I was ready.

Second of all, I didn't think I was qualified.

And thirdly, have you heard some of the questions that 12-year-olds ask?

Thankfully, I accepted the assignment, and the journey began.

When God calls us to do something, it is usually well beyond anything we have ever imagined ourselves doing and it will come at a time when we least expect it.

A lot of times it won't make sense to us or those around us.

Can you imagine how David felt when he was anointed king as a young boy when everyone including his family just thought he was good enough to tend the sheep (1 Samuel 16:11).

What about Abraham, when God told him to just start walking and I'll tell you where you're going when you get there (Genesis 12:1)?

Imagine how Noah must have felt when God told him to start building a giant boat (Genesis 6:14).

What did Elisha think when Elijah saw him plowing the field and cast his mantle upon him (1 Kings 19:19)?

Just think what went through Peter and Andrew's mind when Jesus said, "Come follow Me and I will make you fishers of men" (Matthew 4:19).

What amazes me about these situations is that it doesn't say that any of them hesitated.

Matter of fact it says that Peter and Andrew straightway, or immediately, left their nets and followed Him.

Straightaway.

You want to talk about someone going to the extreme to answer his call?

In 1 Kings 19:21, Elisha took a yoke of oxen and slew them and boiled their flesh with the instruments of the oxen and gave them to the people and they did eat. Then he arose and went after Elijah and ministered unto him.

In other words, Elisha had a cookout using his plow for the fire and his oxen for the burgers. He fed his workers and then he took off following Elijah.

Elisha's actions seem a little extreme at first, but when we unpackage what he did, he is literally going all in.

He is making sure that when he is out there on the road and doubt creeps in, that he won't quit.

When the road gets hard and the enemy starts telling him that he has made a mistake and he is tempted to quit, and he wants to go back to his old life, there won't be anything for him to go back to.

This is Elisha's way of going all in.

It's his way of exercising extreme faith. God if you have called me to be a prophet, then I am no longer a plowboy and I won't need the oxen or the plow ever again.

We can sit here and think that Elisha's behavior is extreme or over the top, or whatever we want to call it, but he is just defeating a temptation that we all have when the road gets hard.

When the path gets tough what is the first thing that we all want to do?

We want to go back to what is comfortable to us. We want to go back to what we know.

This is not exercising faith; it's giving up on it.

The perfect example of this is seen with the disciples in John 21:3. Jesus has been crucified, buried in the tomb, and has resurrected, but He has not ascended to heaven yet.

The disciples don't really know what to do with themselves.

One day Peter says that he is going fishing and some of the others say they will go with him. They fished all night and didn't catch anything.

They tried to go back to who they were before Jesus.

Why didn't they catch anything?

Because they were no longer fishers of fish, they were fishers of men.

Jesus had changed their identity.

When Elisha destroys his plow and oxen, he is just making sure that he doesn't fall to this temptation when the going gets tough.

When we have these moments on our journey, and we will, we must remember that God sees us different than we see ourselves.

When we look at ourselves, all we tend to see is our limits, but God created us, so He sees us with all of our potential.

What I am about to share I believe is the key and the reason most will never realize their full potential. When God created us and put all of that potential inside of us, He placed a condition around it.

A key that unlocks our full potential. You see, our full potential will never be realized by ourselves.

But the limits around our potential disappear when we pursue that potential through a faith in Jesus Christ.

When we apply our faith to our potential, it's like the children of Israel shouting at the walls of Jericho.

They just come tumbling down.

Philippians 4:13, tells us that we can do all things through Christ who strengthens us.

If we can do all things through Christ, then the opposite is also true. This list of things we can accomplish is much shorter without Him.

Because of this truth right here, I won't let my children or church members get away with saying that they can't do something.

I have them rephrase it to, I don't want to do it, or I won't do it, but I won't accept them saying that they can't.

I don't ever want them to place limits on their potential.

With Christ all things are possible.

Not only do we have to get past the limits we place on ourselves, but we have to get past what others think of us too. When others look at us and our potential, they have the habit of placing their limits on us.

In other words, most people will always place themselves above others. If they are not successful at something they don't want to think that anyone else will be either.

They project their limits onto others.

We can't let what others think we can or can't do influence our pursuit of our potential. I don't want to sound arrogant, but when it comes to your abilities and potential, it doesn't matter what others think.

What matters is what you think. And what God knows.

Let's look at some people in the Bible that if others' opinions had mattered their story would have turned out much different.

When God chose David, David's own dad wondered if God had the right kid. When Samuel asked Jesse to bring in his children so he could anoint one, Jesse left David out in the field tending the sheep.

From an outward appearance David didn't look like a mighty king to anyone. But God knew what He had placed inside of David.

When God chose Moses, some of Moses' own people questioned who Moses was. Moses got a little ahead of God and tried to be who he thought God wanted him to be, but the timing wasn't right.

Moses's own people hadn't learned to respect him yet. Also, Moses hadn't learned to lead yet.

When God chose Gideon to lead the army against the Midianites, I wonder how many of the soldiers Gideon chose wondered who Gideon was and what qualified him to lead them into battle.

Gideon didn't have any battle experience.

He hadn't fought in any wars. It doesn't even tell us he was skilled in fighting.

It would be only natural for the men to question his abilities.

What made all of these heroes successful even though it seemed that God had called them to complete impossible tasks, was the fact that they didn't allow what others thought of them to influence their choice to follow God.

They chose to believe God.

Chapter 6

Get Out of The Winepress!

At this point in Gideon's journey to greatness, we have seen God get Gideon to start changing the way he thought of himself.

Gideon is starting to see himself as maybe a little more than just the weakest in the clan. He is starting to think that just maybe he can do more than anyone is giving him credit for.

Gideon is starting to believe in himself.

God has commissioned Gideon with a seemingly impossible task of leading an army into battle against the Midianites.

Furthermore, Gideon is buying into it.

Then just like God, God throws Gideon a curveball.

If you haven't figured it out by now, God has perfected the curveball.

If you know anything about curveballs, they are one of the toughest pitches to hit in baseball.

They start out in one location and when they come across the plate they have moved to another location.

A good hitter learns to recognize the motion of the curve, then he relies on his experience and technique, and then he swings the bat where he anticipates the ball will be to make contact.

When God throws us a curveball, just like that hitter has to rely on his experience and technique, we have to learn to stand on our testimonies from past situations and then exercise our faith in the present situation.

Then just like the batter swings where he expects the ball to be to make contact and get a hit, we are to expect God to show up at the right time and bring us the victory.

This is how Gideon's curveball goes: God sends an angel and tells Gideon that he is not a wimp, that he is a mighty man of valor.

He goes on to tell Gideon that God is wanting him to lead an army against the Midianites.

Once Gideon gets over the shock, he agrees to follow God and do what God has asked.

Here is where the curveball comes.

God says, "You are a mighty man of valor. You are going to lead an army against the Midianites. But first, I want you to go tear down the altars of baal that your father has built and cut down the idols that are next to it" (Judges 6:25).

This is completely different than going into battle against Israel's enemies.

This has to do with righting the wrongs of Israel from the inside first.

And remember, Gideon is a nobody in the eyes of his fellow man.

If Gideon does this, then the men of the city are going to be angry with him and want to kill him.

Why would God do this to Gideon?

This is not just to help Gideon with his fears and to prove to him that God will protect him.

No, the main purpose I believe is to get Gideon out of the winepress.

If the enemy can't see you, then neither can the world.

When God saves us, he doesn't expect us to be camouflage, just the opposite, we are to be visible for everyone to see.

Matter of fact, one of the conditions of God accepting us is the fact that we stand out from the rest of the world.

In 2 Corinthians 6:17, Paul says, "Wherefore come out from among them, and be ye separate, saith the Lord, and touch not the unclean thing; and I will receive you."

God doesn't want us blending in. God is not looking for camouflage believers. He doesn't want us hiding out in the winepress.

Instead, He is looking for just the opposite.

God wants a Kingdom that is easily identified.

He wants His church to be seen. He is looking for a body that will stand out and stand up to the world.

Jesus said it plainly in Matthew 5:14 - 16, "Ye are the light of the world, A city that is set on an hill cannot be hid. Neither do men light a candle, and put it under a bushel, but on a candlestick; and it giveth light unto all that are in the house. Let your light so shine before men, that they may see your good works, and glorify your Father which is in heaven."

Up till now with Gideon, it has been nothing but talk.

No one knows anything about this except God and Gideon.

Gideon has agreed to do this thing that God has called him to do, but he has not really committed to anything yet.

Gideon is still within his safe zone.

God says, "Ok, Gideon. If you're serious, then it's time to prove it. Go tear down the altar to baal and cut down the idols next to it."

God is getting Gideon out of the winepress.

Gideon is making his stand with God and after Gideon tears down the altar, everyone is going to know whose side he is on. Here is where Gideon still plays it safe.

He does what God tells him too, he tears down the altar and cuts down the idols, but he does it at night.

He does what God tells him too, but he still doesn't want to be seen. His fear is still getting the best of him.

How many of us live our lives like this every day? We love the Lord, and we are believers, but when it comes to standing out, we just haven't gotten that far yet.

We don't want to be noticed for our Christianity.

When a co-worker is telling dirty jokes or using foul language, we often just grin and bear it.

Or when someone is spreading gossip or talking bad about someone else, instead of standing up and saying that it's not appropriate behavior, we often just nod in silence. (That's not really agreeing with them, anyways, we justify to ourselves.)

We tell ourselves that it is because we don't want to offend them with our Christianity.

Let's look at the other side of this. When was the last time you prayed for a stranger? When was the last time that you invited someone to church with you?

Again, we tell ourselves that we don't want to be offensive or pushy.

If you saw someone drowning and you had a life ring, would you throw it out to them or would you be afraid that it would offend them?

I understand that it's awkward to ask a stranger if you can pray for them. I understand that sometimes it feels weird inviting someone to church, especially if they knew the old you.

We have to learn to look at it this way: God has given us this life ring and He wants us to throw it.

What is more important? The other person's relationship with God or our feelings?

Just to let you know, in about twenty years of ministry, I can only remember one time where someone turned down prayer and that was because they asked me for money, and I didn't have any to give them.

Also, when it comes to the subject of inviting people to church, I read an article with this caption, "82% of unchurched people are somewhat likely to attend church if invited."

The world needs a church that is not hidden. God has given us the life ring and He expects us to throw it.

Chapter 7

Faith Over Fear (Excuses)

After we accept our God given identity and get over the shock of the assignment, the next step to the Gideon principle is learning to choose faith over fear.

The Gideon principle will not work if we operate from a place of fear.

We must learn to look at every situation through eyes of faith.

The greatest example of this in my mind is found in 2 Kings chapter 6, Elisha and his servant are in the city of Dothan and the king of Syria finds out their location. In the middle of the night, the king sends an army to surround the entire city.

The next morning, when Elisha's servant sees their situation, he is overcome with fear. And He asks Elisha what they are going to do. How will we get out of this?

Elisha's first words to his servant are "fear not: for they that be with us are more than they that be with them". (verse 16).

Elisha then prays to God and asks Him to open the servant's eyes and let him see.

The Lord opened the young man's eyes and he saw that the mountains are full of horses and chariots of fire that are there to fight for Elisha.

What he now saw changed his perspective on the situation. He started out looking through eyes of fear and all he thought about was defeat.

Now he is looking through eyes of faith and realizes that they can't lose.

Gideon was like most of us, letting his fears dictate his actions in his daily life.

One of the first pictures we get of Gideon is him threshing wheat in the winepress.

Threshing wheat is a process that usually requires a lot of room to perform.

So why is Gideon doing this task in the confines of the winepress?

Because he is afraid that the Midianites will see him and show up and steal his harvest. Gideon is viewing the situation through eyes of fear instead of faith.

How we view the situation will dictate the actions with which we approach it.

One thing that all of us are accustomed to when it comes to fear is that it usually stops us from going forward.

We are a lot like Gideon in the winepress. It stops us from being successful or achieving what we have set out to do.

It stops us from putting in for that promotion at work. It stops us from chasing our dreams of opening our own business.

Not only will fear stop us from going forward with life changing things in our lives, but fear will also stop us from things that are not so big and life changing.

Like the fear of what people think will stop you from singing in the choir at church.

How many times has the fear of public speaking stopped us from sharing our testimony or the fear of a stranger thinking we are some religious nut, if we are impressed to pray for them in public?

How many times do we let the fear of failure keep us on the sidelines?

Fear will rob us of life's experiences.

When I was growing up and would go through a period of fear and anxiety, my dad had a saying he would use.

He would tell me, "You can get busy living, or you can get busy dying."

He was not being mean at all.

He just realized that my fears were crippling me when it came to the experiences of life.

He also realized that I was the only one who could do anything about the situation.

What if I told you that letting our fears hinder us is exactly what the enemy wants, so that we fail, but that God wants us to allow our fears to motivate us to be successful.

In other words, instead of letting our fears hold us back, we need to learn to let them launch us forward.

I want to be like David when it comes to the bear and the lion. I want to be the one doing the chasing.

When it comes to facing the giants of life, I want to run to meet them like David ran to meet Goliath. Does that mean that the fear or the anxiety doesn't exist, no not at all?

It just means that we have learned to use it as an ally to move us forward instead of an obstacle that holds us back. The only difference between courage and fear is who is in control.

Fear says that the enemy is in control.

Courage says that God is in control.

I have two teenage sons who are pretty decent when it comes to baseball.

My oldest son, Elijah, has always been cool under pressure. He controls his nerves well and you can hardly tell if anything rattles him when he is on the ballfield.

My youngest son, Ethan, is a little different story.

Ethan wears his emotions on his sleeve. He doesn't hold anything in. I am not saying this is a good or bad thing. It is just his personality.

Elijah and Ethan are opposites when it comes to this, and they have to learn to apply their faith in different ways. The method might be different, but the answer is the same.

Ethan is a pretty good hitter, but he didn't start out that way.

He went through a phase where he didn't want to bat because he was afraid that he would get hit with the ball.

Not only did this fear keep him from being successful but it promoted bad habits like bailing out or pulling back before the ball got to the plate.

Anyone that knows anything about baseball knows that you can't hit the ball if you are running from it.

Well, we can apply the same principle to life. You can't overcome any problems if you are running from them.

Not only does fear produce hesitation and hinder us from moving forward, but fear is also a breeding ground for excuses.

Over and over, throughout scripture, we see people come up with excuse after excuse when they are afraid of something God gives them to do.

Moses tells God that he can't speak well when God tells him to go before Pharaoh.

Jeremiah tells God that he is just a boy when God calls him to be a prophet unto the nations.

Gideon's excuse is he is the least of his clan.

How come when it comes to service in the kingdom when we are asked to do something, the first thing that comes out of our mouth is an excuse to why we can't instead of reason as to why we can.

Throughout the course of pastoring, I've heard many excuses from I'm too busy, to I've done my time, to I can't do that, to I don't want other people to be upset.

All these are just excuses for fears that we don't want to admit to or mixed-up priorities that we need to address.

If anyone in the Bible had a good excuse to miss Jesus, it was Zacchaeus.

In Luke 19, we read of the story where Jesus was passing through Jericho. Zacchaeus was a rich businessman in the city, and he desired to see Jesus as He passed by, but he couldn't.

He was too short to see over the crowd.

Now Zacchaeus could have made the excuse that he was too short to see Jesus as He came by, but he didn't. Instead, just the opposite, he found a way to make sure that he saw Jesus.

Zacchaeus found a sycamore tree and he climbed up the tree so that he could see over everyone and see Jesus.

Zacchaeus was a sinner and he put everything to the side just to catch a glimpse of Jesus.

He didn't care what people thought. He didn't care if people laughed. He didn't care if people talked about him. He made no excuses, he wanted to see Jesus.

When Jesus came to that tree, He stopped and called Zacchaeus down and told Zacchaeus that He must abide in his house.

Because Zacchaeus made no excuses, he found the favor of the Lord.

Our fears, if allowed to control us, will weaken our faith, and cause us to doubt God.

Fear will cause us to make excuses that will disappoint God and fear will cause us to fail before we even try.

We have to learn to overcome fears and the most effective way to do this is to exercise our faith!

Chapter 8

Fleecing God (Being Sure)

So far, with the Gideon principle, we have seen Gideon hear from God. We've seen him realize his identity in God compared to the world and put his fears and excuses behind him.

Next, we see him do something that will get different opinions based on who you talk to.

Some think Gideon's next action was an insult to God.

I don't see it that way. I see it as Gideon making sure that he didn't miss or misunderstand God.

God tells Gideon that He is going to deliver the Israelites from the Midianites by using Gideon to lead them into battle.

When Gideon hears this, he immediately begins to question God.

Gideon wants to know that God didn't make a mistake. Remember God sees us different than we see ourselves.

At this point, Gideon might believe that God has something great for him, but he is still not so sure that he is the mighty man of valor that God has called him.

So, what Gideon does next is leave no doubt that he is hearing from God. He places a fleece before God.

Some people may think that Gideon was challenging God.

I don't.

I think Gideon was just being certain.

Gideon says, "God, if You are truly going to do this thing that You have spoken through me, then I will place a fleece out on the ground tonight and in the morning let the fleece be wet with dew and the ground all around it be dry" (Judges 6:36-38).

God delivers exactly what Gideon asks for. The next morning, Gideon takes the fleece and wrings a bowl of water out of it while the ground all around it is dry.

Well, true to his nature, Gideon, still is not convinced that God is going to do what He is saying.

So, he asked God again, "God, if You are really going to do this then let me put the fleece out before You one more time, only this time, in the morning let the fleece be dry and the ground all around it be wet with dew" (Judges 6:39-40).

Gideon gets up the next morning and finds that God has done exactly as he has asked. The fleece is dry and the ground all around is wet.

There was no way in the world that Gideon could have mistaken that God had done exactly what he had asked of Him.

God had taken away any doubt that Gideon might have had.

For those of us that need God to speak to us through a big neon sign, we can completely relate to how Gideon felt.

When I was answering the call the Lord had placed on my life to preach and pastor, I had a similar experience with God, except instead of it being a physical fleece, it was more of a mental, spiritual fleece.

I had already preached for the first time and had been given a second date to preach again.

About 2 weeks before this I had finished reading the book of Isaiah in my daily studying. I decided I would not start the next book until after I had preached this next message.

I was going to give all of my energy and time the next 2 weeks to prepare this message.

Well, just let me say it was probably one of the toughest 2-week periods in all of my nearly twenty years of ministry.

The enemy was constantly barraging my mind with thoughts like I wasn't good enough, I was missing God, God can't and won't use someone like me. I was doing it for myself and not the Lord.

Then, on top of those thoughts, Letisha and I couldn't get along for nothing.

It just seemed like everything was a constant struggle and battle.

The night before I was supposed to preach it came to a head within myself.

I had had all I could stand. I remember looking up and telling the Lord that I quit. I give up, there is no way I can battle the devil, my wife, and everything else.

If God was really calling me to do this, then He had to let me know without a doubt, if not I would preach the next day because I had committed to it, but after that I was finished.

I went to spend some time in prayer and while I was praying, I remember the Lord impressing in my spirit, just like He was talking to me.

He said, "Read where you should be reading".

I didn't realize that the next book of the Bible that I would start was Jeremiah, but I responded to the Lord with, "Ok God when I get done praying, I will read two chapters."

In the next few minutes, I finished up praying and took my Bible and walked into the living room of our house.

Something on the television caught my eye and I laid my Bible down on the ottoman and started watching T.V.

Only a few minutes passed by. Stronger than before, God impressed again upon my spirit, and this is what I heard, "I said, read where you should be reading."

This got my attention. I said, "OK Lord, I will read one chapter."

I don't even think I finished the chapter.

I got to verse 4 and I knew that God had heard my cry and He was answering my prayer.

God was speaking directly to me through the pages of the Bible.

This is what it said, "Then the word of the Lord came unto me, saying, Before I formed thee in the belly I knew thee; and before thou camest forth out of the womb I sanctified thee, and I ordained thee a prophet unto the nations" (Jeremiah 1:5).

There it was.

God had answered my fleece and I didn't even realize that I had placed it before Him.

Yet from that moment on, I have never questioned my call to be a preacher or a pastor.

I have let my steps be ordered by the Lord and anytime the enemy tries to get me to doubt my call, or anyone comes at me about what I am doing, I just go back to that moment where I know that God spoke directly to me.

All doubt that has crept in disappears and is replaced with certainty.

You can't tell me that many times on the battlefield doubt and uncertainty didn't creep up in the back of Gideons mind.

He would hear the voices, "You missed God, who do you think you are, you are never going to win, you are responsible for all of these people that are following you and they are going to see you fail."

When Gideon would find himself in these low moments during battle all he had to do was remind himself of the fleece that he had placed before God.

God had directly answered him and promised that Gideon was going to be victorious.

There is nothing that can compare to knowing that God has spoken directly to you.

There is a difference in questioning God and making sure of your call.

Chapter 9

God's Ways Are Not Our Ways

This part of the Gideon Principle right here is where we really see one of the infinite characteristics of God.

So many times, throughout this ministry, I have seen God work in situations in ways that no one would ever think of.

I would think that I had it all figured out that this way or that way was the only way that God could fix something only to have Him work it out in a way that I never in a million years would have seen coming.

I have seen Him restore relationships that I thought were certainly over when no human assistance seemed to help.

I have seen people raised up off of their deathbeds when all medical knowledge had been exhausted. I have seen Him deliver drug addicts with no medical intervention whatsoever.

I have witnessed situation after situation where the outcome could only be explained with the words "but God!"

It is these times of utter amazement that we see the words of Ephesians 3:20 come to life right before our eyes.

Ephesians 3:20 says that He is able to do exceedingly abundantly above all we can ask or think.

In other words, God is telling us that He can and will do things that we can't understand or explain.

So many of us limit God's abilities in our lives by trying to understand or explain how He works.

Exercising our faith in God is when we accept the outcome of a situation without having to explain it or understand it.

In reality, which do you care more about: that God hears and answers your prayers, or the process in which He answered your prayers?

After his ordeal was over, Jonah didn't ask God why the whale swallowed him (Jonah 1:17). He was just glad it did.

Peter didn't ask Jesus how he was able to walk on water (Matthew 14:28-29). He was just glad he could.

The blind man didn't get angry at Jesus for spitting in his eyes (Mark 8:22-26). He was just glad that He did.

You get the point.

Earlier in Chapter 2, we quoted Isaiah 55:8 which tells us that His thoughts are not our thoughts, and His ways are not our ways.

This is just a fancy way of saying we can't figure Him out.

The reason we can't figure Him out is because He operates above human limits and abilities. As humans we operate in the realm of what is possible.

When it comes to God, He is the one who decides what is possible.

God doesn't want us to figure Him out.

He wants us to trust Him.

Before we look at Gideon's situation, let's look at some other situations in the Bible that humanly don't make sense. But the people trusted God and they saw Him move mightily.

The first one I think of is Samson.

He is about to take on an army of Philistines and he has no weapon. He looks around and finds the jawbone of a donkey. Samson takes that jawbone and defeats one thousand Philistines (Judges 15:14-15).

We have talked about David earlier in this book. It doesn't make sense that he, being just a teenage boy, defeated Goliath, a mighty warrior with just a slingshot and a stone (1 Samuel 17:49-50).

It doesn't make sense that the disciples fished all night and caught nothing but then Jesus tells them to cast on the other side of the boat and they pull in a haul that rips their nets (John 21:3-11).

It doesn't make sense that when it comes time to pay the temple tax, Jesus tells Peter to go fishing and when he catches a fish to get the coin out of its mouth and go pay the tax (Matthew 17:27).

One more before we look at Gideon: the woman with the issue of blood (Luke 8:43-48).

For twelve years she had gone to doctor after doctor and spent all of her money trying to find a cure.

She finds herself desperate with almost all of her hope gone.

The only hope she has left is that she hears that Jesus is passing through. She thinks, "if I can just touch His clothes then I will be healed".

Now I don't know where she came up with that idea, maybe she had heard stories about it happening to others.

All she knew is nothing else worked and she was desperate. She pushed her way through the crowd, and she was able to just barely touch the hem of His garment.

She was instantly healed.

This makes no human sense whatsoever, except that He was Jesus, and His ways are not our ways.

She didn't care how she was healed. She was just glad she was.

Look what Jesus says to the woman in Luke 8:48, "Daughter be of good comfort: thy faith hath made the whole; go in peace."

There is the key again.

Jesus said that her faith had made her whole. It didn't matter that no one else believed she would be healed.

It didn't matter that it didn't make sense to anyone else, it didn't even matter that she didn't understand. Or that it didn't make sense to her.

What mattered was that her faith was in Jesus.

She didn't need an explanation; she needed an answer and that is what her faith brought her.

Let's look at Gideon's situation.

Gideon has accepted God's assignment. He has overcome his fear. He has fleeced God and is willing to lead an army against the Midianites.

Gideon does what makes sense to me from a military point of view. He goes and starts gathering his army. He gathers up 32,000 that are with him (Judges 7:1-7).

Now keep in mind that they are about to take on 435,000 Midianites, so even though 32,000 is a lot, they are still vastly outnumbered.

Well, God speaks to Gideon and tells him that he has too many people with him.

God tells him to send all of the ones that are fearful and afraid home.

Gideon does this and 22,000 of those with Gideon leave. This leaves 10,000 left with Gideon to fight the Midianites.

Now if I am Gideon, I would be nervous taking on 435,000 with 32,000, but now God has sent 22,000 away and Gideon has lost ⅔ of his army.

If I am Gideon this probably is the part of me where human nature takes over and I start to question God.

Well God being God – He tells Gideon, "you still have too many, we have to get rid of some more of them".

Not only does the fact that God is taking numbers away from Gideon not make human sense, but the method with which He picks those that go and fight with Gideon is hard to understand also.

The way I would go about picking a small group of soldiers that were going to fight alongside me and take on a great army would go something like this.

I would set up different contests to see who the best and the strongest were.

I would have created an arrow shooting contest. I would have held a sword wielding contest. We could have held all sorts of strength and speed contests to see who the greatest warriors were.

Doesn't that seem like the best way to find the best fighting men?

Guess what? Just like I said earlier, God doesn't do things the way I think He will.

He tells Gideon to bring those that are left down to the water, and He will choose which ones will go with Gideon.

God told Gideon to separate them according to the way they drank water. Here again is something that doesn't make human sense to me.

A whopping 9,700 bowed down on their knees to drink water. The other 300 used their hands to pull the water up to their mouths to drink.

God told Gideon to take those 300 into battle with him.

So now Gideon has his army of 300 and he is about ready to take on the massive Midianite army.

Now if any of this still makes human sense, what's left is about to go flying out the window.

I would think if God only gave me 300 to take on such a massive army that He was going to make us invincible or infuse us with superhuman powers or something like that.

Three hundred against 435,000 makes no sense at all and seems completely impossible for Gideon to win.

Yet when God is on our side, we are never outnumbered.

Did God make Gideon's army invincible?

Did God infuse them with superpowers?

The answer is no, but what He did is even more incredible than any of that.

Matter of fact it is exceedingly abundantly above what any of us could ever think. (You like what I did there?)

God told Gideon for all of the men to get some torches and place pitchers over them. They were to take the torches and pitchers in one hand and a trumpet in the other hand.

You read that right.

The Lord told Gideon to take 300 men and leave their swords and bows and arrows at home.

He told Gideon to give them torches and pitchers and trumpets and go take on an army of 435,000.

I can almost hear Gideon say out loud, "Lord, this makes absolutely no sense at all, and I don't see how in the world we are going to win, but nevertheless I will follow You!"

You know what happened, Gideon divided his men up and placed them around the Midianites at night and they blew the trumpets, broke the pitchers, and shouted, "The sword of the Lord and of Gideon."

The Midianites didn't have a clue what was going on. The Lord caused them to turn on themselves with their swords and Gideon won a great victory.

When it comes to the way the Lord works, we can always look at the who's, the why's and the how's, but if we really have faith in the Lord and want to see His will be done, does any of that really matter.

Those questions and doubts are not worth missing the mighty and miraculous works of God.

Could we have promised the same outcome if Gideon had done things his way?

Probably not.

We have to learn and trust the Lord and follow Him even when things don't make sense, or we don't understand.

Chapter 10

God Did His Homework

My journey to being a pastor was almost as crazy as Gideon's road to victory.

Most of the time we would think that pastors go to seminary or get official training when it comes to pastoring.

But this was not what the Lord had in mind for me.

First of all, I am not what you would call a great student. I didn't make bad grades, I just struggled applying myself in that type of environment. I have nothing against education and I, myself, love to learn.

I just do better learning at my own pace in an environment that is not rigid or time sensitive.

The Lord knew this about me, and I had to learn to trust Him during the process of answering my calling. You will understand what I mean shortly.

Earlier I shared with you Jeremiah 1:5 when I was struggling to find my call to preach. How when God led me to this verse, I knew God had heard my cry and I have never questioned my calling since that moment.

Just to remind you, this is what the verse says, "Before I formed thee in the belly I knew thee; and before thou camest forth out of the womb I sanctified thee, and I ordained thee a prophet unto the nations."

Now, what if I told you that that verse right there applied to everyone?

Just like Jeremiah received the certainty of his calling through this verse, and I received the certainty of my calling through this verse, so can you.

There is another verse that I want to share with you right here that will give us more insight into God's character, and it will activate Jeremiah 1:5 for us.

Acts 10:34, "Then Peter opened his mouth and said, Of the truth I perceive that God is no respecter of persons."

Wow, this right here is an incredible scripture. It simply means that God has no favorites.

In other words, He doesn't give one-person special opportunities and then block others from having them. It doesn't matter our race, our nationality, or our economic status.

It doesn't even matter our age.

He used David as a young teenager to take down a giant and He used Caleb at 80 years of age to conquer a mountain.

God doesn't discriminate.

If He has a plan for my life, then He has a plan for your life. The only prerequisite is that we have to surrender our lives to Him.

Now who is ready to get off that couch and climb some mountains and slay some giants?

You might be thinking that you believe that God has called you to something, but a prophet unto the nations you know is not your calling.

Guess what? You are probably right.

Not everyone is called to be a mighty prophet like Jeremiah or an Evangelist like the apostle Paul. Not everyone is called to a formal church ministry like I am.

But everyone is called to something.

That is the beauty of the scripture Jeremiah 1:5. The first part of the scripture, "Before I formed thee in the belly I knew thee; and before thou camest forth out of the womb I sanctified thee…"

That part of the scripture is for everyone; it doesn't change.

Before we were ever a glimmer in our parents' eyes, God knew everything about us.

Then He goes on and says that He sanctified us. That word sanctified means that He set us apart for something. He had a plan for us before we were ever born.

Here is the powerful thing about this scripture, the last part, where it says, "and I ordained thee a prophet unto the nations".

This part of the scripture is like a fill in the blank depending on who God is talking to.

At the time where it says, "a prophet unto the nations", He was talking with Jeremiah. When He assured me of being called to the ministry, He was talking with me.

When it comes to you, it may say business owner, doctor, lawyer, or banker.

Or, it might say factory worker, waitress, or truck driver. The beauty of it is that God doesn't need 7 billion pastors or 7 billion evangelists. He needs people that are willing to minister and share the gospel in all walks of life.

He needs people that will minister at the bus station. He needs people that will minister in the grocery store. He needs people that will minister in the factories.

He needs people that will minister in restaurants. He needs people that will minister in the hospitals.

I think you get the point.

Then He also needs people that will organize and lead them when they come together and form a local church.

Are you ready to answer your call?

Where do I begin?

I know that is what I would ask myself!

I started out by talking to people that were over me in the Lord.

I felt like God was calling me to preach. But I wasn't even close to being sure, so I talked to other preachers. I would ask them how they knew they were called.

Usually none of them could give me a definitive hard answer because everyone's journey is different.

What I've learned over the past 20 years and where I would advise anyone to begin to answer their call, would be to look at your life's experiences.

What has God brought you through?

One thing I have learned with God is that He doesn't waste experiences.

There is always a point to them, whether it is to strengthen us or to test our faith, or prepare us for the next battle, and so on.

Just like David said, he was qualified to fight Goliath because while he was tending sheep, a lion and a bear had come to kill some, and he chased them down and slew them.

David realized that this was God's doing because he goes on to tell king Saul that just like God delivered the lion and the bear into his hand, He would do the same thing when it came to Goliath (1 Samuel 17:33-37).

This is the same way that God works in each of us.

I didn't surrender my life to the Lord until I was 27 years old. I was married and pretty much just concerned about making money.

I worked for one of the largest trucking companies in the nation and seemed to have a pretty promising future with them.

So, when I did surrender my life to the Lord, pastoring or going back to school was the furthest thing from my mind.

Well, like I've have said many times throughout this book so far, God had other plans.

I didn't realize it, at the time, but God had been preparing me my whole life for my Gideon moment. He had been preparing me for the time that I would answer His call.

There are many times since becoming a pastor that I have sat and reflected over the experiences in my life and can see how God was using that moment or that experience to train me for what I would face in pastoring.

I grew up on a farm and I can't count all the lessons that I was taught right there alone. We raised tobacco as a cash crop. We cut and sold firewood, and we maintained around 30 head of beef cattle.

The first thing that I will tell you I learned is hard work. When it comes to ministry, if you are scared of hard work, then it might not be your calling.

The second thing I will tell you I learned is that farming never takes a day off. There is something to do every day.

Those animals depend on you every day of the week and it's not always convenient. They have to eat when it's raining, they have to eat when it's snowing, they need you when it's hot and when it's cold.

You might have some days that are easier than others, but very rarely will you ever get to take a day off on the farm.

Guess what? It is the same when it comes to ministry.

Ministry is rarely convenient and there is always something that needs to be done. So, if you are thinking about going into ministry because you think it's easy, think again.

Make sure that it's your calling.

My best friend's dad was our county 4-H agent and I got involved because of my friend. We would raise sheep every year.

We would get them as little lambs and raise them for a few months and then we would take them to a few shows, and we would end up in Nashville every summer. After the Nashville show, we would sell them and usually make, what was some decent money to us kids.

To be honest, my motive was to get to go to Nashville and to make some money, but can I tell you that the lessons that I learned from dealing with those sheep and the experiences I got through 4-H, I use regularly in pastoring.

As I said earlier, I worked for one of the largest trucking companies in America making pretty good money when God called me to preach.

This was a secular company that had nothing to do with church or ministry, but I learned so much about managing people and treating people fairly and I could go on and on, but I won't bore you.

The point is everything that you have been through. Every mountain that you have climbed and every pit that you have fell into, God will not waste that experience.

He will take it and if you let Him, He will use it to shape you and prepare you for what He has called you to do.

All those times where you messed up and you just want to forget about, he can use them. We will look at that more in depth in the next chapter.

Chapter 11

You're Not a Victim

In the last chapter we talked about how God will use our past experiences to train us for future situations.

He uses the good and the bad, the mountaintops and the valleys. The truth is we don't mind Him using the mountaintop experiences, but we struggle when it comes to the valleys.

A lot of people when they find themselves in those valleys develop a victim mentality. They start questioning God as to why them?

They start passing blame of the situation on others. They start complaining as to how life isn't fair, and they don't deserve what they are going through.

Look with me back to when the angel first shows up, we see Gideon fall into this trap.

Judges 6:13, "And Gideon said unto him, Oh my Lord, if the Lord be with us, why then is all this befallen us? And where be all His miracles which our fathers told us of, saying, Did not the Lord bring us up from Egypt? But now the Lord Hath forsaken us and delivered us into the hands of the Midianites."

I can just see Gideon giving the angel this response very sarcastically: "If I am a mighty man of valor and God is who our fathers say He is, then why in the world is all of this negative stuff happening to us? Not only has God abandoned us, but He has delivered us into the hands of the Midianites."

Gideon is playing the pity card. He is blaming God for the situation that they are in.

He never stopped to think that the reason they may be in that situation is because they turned their backs on God.

I have never read anywhere in the Bible where God says that we are victims.

Just the opposite.

He says that we are more than conquerors (Romans 8:37).

We are the head and not the tail (Deuteronomy 28:13).

And then, probably the most powerful one, Revelation 12:11, says that we are overcomers by the blood of the Lamb and the word of our testimony.

None of these statements are conditional to any situation. They are simply who God says that we are.

You got fired from work? You are an overcomer.

You got diagnosed with cancer? You are an overcomer.

You got passed over for that promotion? You're the head and not the tail.

Your business deal fell through? Guess what, you are still the head and not the tail.

Maybe someone lied to you and took advantage of you. You're not a victim!

You're an overcomer by the blood of the lamb and the word of your testimony.

Maybe you're like me and have suffered off and on from anxiety.

Listen to me, you are not a victim.

God is not picking on you.

You are an overcomer by the blood of the Lamb and the word of your testimony!

Let me show you what I mean.

In Genesis 50:20, we see Joseph proclaim to his brothers, "But as for you, ye though evil against me; but God meant it unto good, to bring to pass, as it is this day, to save much people alive."

I think if anyone had the right to proclaim that he was a victim or that he was treated unfairly, it had to be Joseph.

Yet not one time in the story of Joseph do we ever see him complain about his situation or get mad at God.

If anyone had a right to be bitter and say that life was unfair, it was Joseph. His story starts out that he is his father's favorite child.

This already puts Joseph at odds when it comes to his brothers.

Then Joseph has two dreams and, in these dreams, his family, all his brothers, even his mother and father bow down before Joseph.

Joseph is excited and shares his dream with his family. As you can imagine, they are not too thrilled.

One day when the brothers are off tending the flocks, Joseph's father, Jacob, sends Joseph to see about his brothers.

His brothers, realizing their opportunity, take Joseph and place him in a pit.

They strip him of his coat, dip it in blood and tell their father that a wild animal killed him.

The brothers then take Joseph and sell him to some slave traders. Joseph is sold to Potiphar who is captain of Pharaoh's guard.

Even though Joseph was a slave, God was with him, and Joseph found favor in Potiphar's sight.

Potiphar promoted Joseph to oversee his entire household.

After some time passed, Potiphar's wife started to desire Joseph and make advances towards him. When Joseph refused, Potiphar's wife lied about Joseph and accused him of having his way with her. Potiphar had Joseph thrown in prison.

This is the second time we see someone do Joseph wrong, yet still no complaining or claiming to be a victim.

Guess what, while Joseph was in prison, the Lord was with him, and Joseph found favor with the warden and soon was placed in charge of the other prisoners.

Two of Pharaoh's servants, the chief baker, and the chief cupbearer, had offended Pharaoh and found themselves in prison with Joseph. While they were in prison, they both had dreams and Joseph interpreted them for them.

The outcome of the dreams was that in three days the chief cupbearer would be reinstated but the baker would be hanged. Joseph asked the cup bearer to remember him when he was reinstated but he forgot about Joseph.

Things happened just like Joseph said they would, yet Joseph was forgotten about until Pharaoh himself had two dreams that troubled him. The chief cupbearer then remembered Joseph and Pharaoh sent for him. Joseph interpreted the dream that there was going to be seven years of plenty and then seven years of famine.

Joseph was promoted to second in command of Egypt, only Pharaoh ranked above him. When the seven years of famine came, people from all over came to Egypt because Joseph had stored up grain and prepared for the famine.

This is how Joseph's brothers wound up before him.

They were starving and they came to buy grain. Joseph could have easily gotten revenge on them for what they did to him. He could have turned them away and let them starve, but he realized that everything he had been through was all part of God's plan.

He realized that everything he had been through was bigger than Him. He understood that all things happen to the good to them that love God, to them that are called according to his purpose.

We have to learn to look at our negative situations through eyes of faith.

Instead of looking at it like we are the victims and being treated unfairly we need to learn to look for God in the situation.

Just like He was with Joseph in the pit and in the prison, He will be with us every step of the way.

If we find ourselves in a tough season and we are doing everything that we know to do, odds are that God is either preparing us or positioning us for something great!

I am not Joseph.

And I can't even begin to tell you that I have gone through everything he did, but there is one instance in my life that I went through that taught me that not everything is as it seems.

Sometimes there are greater lessons to learn. I shared earlier with you that I used to work for one of the largest trucking companies in America.

I worked there for over nine years and while I was there, I learned many valuable lessons, but none more valuable than the one I am about to share.

This lesson has helped me time after time throughout the course of my pastorate.

I can directly affect how someone treats me by the way I react to them.

In other words, I can control the situation, or I can react to the situation.

While working for this trucking company, I started out as the 29th part timer on the list and I worked my way up to a dock supervisor by the time I left.

During my time as a dock supervisor, I had four Operations Managers that I would work under depending on which one was working on a typical day.

Three of the operations managers I got along with fairly well and didn't have too many problems, but there was this one that I just didn't get along with at all.

He didn't like me.

And to tell you the truth, I didn't like him that much either.

We disliked each other so much that it was a joke around the workplace.

Everyone knew that if we got close to each other there was a good chance that an explosion could occur.

We would just pop off to each other or say something smart to each other. It went on for so long that that is what we came to expect of each other.

One Saturday morning we were working, and I guess he was in a bad mood and just needed to relieve some pressure.

So, here he came walking through my section and found something wrong and lit into me.

Well, me not being able to keep my mouth shut and thinking that I was being mistreated, I started firing back.

It quickly escalated to the point where I told him that if that was the way it was going to be that I was just going to go home.

Now listen to me, I was saved at this point, but I couldn't see anything that God was doing.

I was miserable.

I felt like God was calling me into full time ministry, but He wasn't opening any doors. I didn't realize it at the time, but God was teaching and preparing for when He would open that door.

When I told him that I was going home and started walking towards the parking lot, the Operations Manager came to me and got me to stay the rest of the day.

I stayed and we just kept our distance from each other.

Well even though that was one of the worst times we had ever gotten into it, I thought it was over just like all the other times.

Boy, was I wrong!

That following Monday just before quitting time, a voice came over the loudspeaker calling me to the terminal manager's office.

This was the big boss.

I knew immediately something was up. I walked in and there sat the Operations Manager that I had gotten into it with, along with some other management people.

I sat down and the terminal manager tore into me.

He got onto me for being insubordinate and this and that. He was telling me how close to being fired that I had come.

All the while he was not saying anything to the manager that I had gotten into it with.

This guy had cussed me and yelled at me in front of other workers, and nothing was being said to him.

It looked like they were blaming everything on me.

Even though I was fuming inside, I just kept my mouth shut and took it. When I left that office, I guess I was more confused than ever.

I stewed over it for days.

God, I am trying to do my best and when other people mistreat me, it's my fault.

God, I don't get it. That's when God said this to me.

This is the lesson He was teaching me: "You're not responsible for the actions of others, you're only responsible for how you act."

Man, that hit me like a ton of bricks. I began to reflect over what had happened and I began to realize that even though he had treated me wrong, I hadn't displayed the best set of actions either.

Just because I had been treated wrong didn't give me an excuse to lower the standard of my actions.

For days I not only reflected on that situation, but I began to reflect back on how I had treated him in the past.

What I found was that I hadn't always treated him like my supervisor and given him the respect that his position deserved.

This was a tough lesson for me to learn.

A few weeks go by and then the opportunity presents itself. I find myself alone right outside the office with this guy.

I approached him and called his name and he responded with a sarcastic, "What do you want?" I told him that I owed him an apology and that I wanted to apologize.

I told him that I had not always respected him like I had my other supervisors and that I had worked harder for them than I did him.

I told him from now on that would not be the case, that whether we like each other or not, I was going to work as hard for him as I did any of the other supervisors.

I stayed true to my word.

How he treated me no longer impacted how I treated him or how I performed my job duties.

You wouldn't believe it, but his demeanor towards me completely changed. From that point on we got along great, we were never best friends, but from time to time we actually joked around with each other.

Even after I left working there, if I called back over there and he answered the phone, he would always ask how I was doing and how my family was doing.

When I decided that I was no longer the victim and started to take responsibility for my actions and change them in the situation, it changed the whole situation.

Also, it wasn't too long after I learned this lesson, that God opened that door for me to step into full time ministry.

Sometimes we think we are waiting on God when, in reality, He is waiting on us.

Chapter 12

Your Latter Will Be Greater

Until David killed Goliath everyone just thought he was a little shepherd boy.

Until Moses brought Israel out of Egyptian bondage most looked at him like he was just living the best of both worlds since he had been raised by Pharaoh's daughter.

Until it started raining, most people thought Noah was crazy for building a boat in the wilderness.

Until Gideon defeated the Midianites, most people thought he was just a little wimpy farmer.

I wonder who all looked at Jesus' disciples and thought Andrew, Peter, James, and John are just fishermen, Matthew is just a government worker, and Peter is a Zealot and an anarchist.

How are they going to change the world??

Then what about those that looked at Jesus Himself and thought isn't that just Joseph's son a carpenter, what's so special about Him?

I want to tell you people won't remember you for how you start out, what will count and what they will remember about you is how you finish.

David might have started out as a little shepherd boy, but he is remembered as a giant killer.

Moses might have started out being orphaned and raised by pharaoh's daughter, but he is remembered as one of the greatest leaders in the history of Israel.

Noah may have started out with people thinking he was crazy and making fun of him, but they thought he was a genius when the flood came.

Gideon might have started out as a wimp, but he is remembered as a mighty warrior.

Jesus might have started as a baby in a manger, He went out on a cross on top of Calvary's hill, but He is not finished yet.

He is coming back as the King of kings and the Lord of lords!

Matter of fact when it comes to Gideon, look how the people respond to him in Judges 8:22, "Then the men of Israel said unto Gideon, Rule over us, both thou and thy son, and thy son's son also for thou hast delivered us from the hand of Midian."

This is incredible.

Just a short time earlier Gideon was the butt of jokes, he was the least of the weakest clan, hiding from the enemy.

Now, suddenly, after Gideon hears from and follows God, the men of Israel want him to be king and rule over them.

You want to talk about a turnaround?!?!

That is greater than Michael Jordan being cut from his high school basketball team and then going on to become the greatest basketball player ever.

That is greater than Colonel Sanders pitching his chicken recipe and getting rejected 1009 times before anyone took a chance on him.

It's greater than Walt Disney who was rejected 302 times for the financing of his dream Disney world. When the world said no to them, they chose not to believe the world.

These men, and many other men and women just like them, chose to believe that they were more than what the world said they were.

When Gideon had to make a choice, he chose to believe the angel of the Lord instead of the world.

Jeremiah 29:11, says, "That I know the plans that I have for you, declares the Lord, plans to prosper you and not to harm you, plans to give you hope and a future."

These are plans He has had for us before we were ever born.

Remember that.

What an awesome God that, before we were ever born, He laid out plans for us that were full of prosperity and hope.

Now don't get me wrong, I don't believe that this means that God wants everyone of us to be millionaires, have a house on every continent and drive a different car each week.

But I do believe that He wants us to live a life free of fear and bondage to the things of this world.

I do believe that He wants each of us to achieve greatness.

And I do believe that if we wholeheartedly trust Him and place our faith in Him, I believe that we will accomplish greater things than we could ever imagine.

One more thing that we need to understand about the Gideon principle is that <u>it is a process.</u>

I do believe God wants us to achieve great things. I do believe that we were created for greatness, and I do believe that God's plans for us are good.

But I don't believe it comes easy and I don't believe it happens all at once.

Haggai 2:9, says, "The glory of this latter house shall be greater than of the former…"

What this is saying is that the ending is going to be greater than the beginning.

Can I tell you what is so powerful about this?

When it comes to our relationship with God, it doesn't matter how we started out, what matters is how we finish.

God never called Gideon a wimp because God wasn't looking at his beginning.

He was looking at how Gideon would finish.

God never called David a ruddy little shepherd boy, instead He called him a man after His own heart, why, you guessed it; God wasn't looking at how he started, He was looking at how he would finish.

Here is the kicker, from the starting point of a race to the ending point of a race, there is a space of distance. The winner of the race is not determined by who starts out the best or even who makes it halfway in the best time.

No, the winner is determined by who covers the whole distance in the fastest time.

When it comes to our beginning point and our ending point with God, our race is not measured in distance, it is measured in time.

So, there is not just one winner like a race that covers distance, but what measures how well we do in our race is how well we steward that time.

What do we cultivate with that time?

Do we spend it in the winepress hiding from the enemy or do we spend it covered in the armor of God fighting the good fight of faith?

Moses didn't start out as the great leader of Israel that delivered them from Egyptian bondage, no he had to first spend 40 years in the wilderness.

David didn't start out a mighty giant killer, no he first had to kill a lion and a bear. Gideon didn't start out as a great prophet of God, no he first had to learn to trust God and follow God when it didn't always make sense.

We can look at each of these and say what makes their latter greater is how they turned out.

We can see how they progressed, and how God promoted them.

Moses became the leader because he trusted God, David became a giant killer because he trusted God and Gideon became a great prophet because he trusted God.

What makes our latter greater is the presence of God.

When it comes to Haggai 2:9, we usually stop halfway through. We stop with the "latter part of this house shall be greater than the former", but the scripture doesn't end there.

Why will the latter be greater than the former?

The scripture ends with this, "...and in this place will I give peace, saith the Lord of hosts." The Lord Himself is going to establish a presence in the house.

When the Lord shows up, things begin to change. Nothing compares to the presence of the Lord.

David tells us in Psalm 16:11, "That Thou wilt show me the path of life: in thy presence is fulness of joy; at thy right hand there are pleasures for evermore."

David had learned to trust God in every circumstance because he had learned that He was always in God's presence. He came to know that God would not leave him or forsake him.

What made David great was the presence of God. What made Moses great was the presence of God and what made Gideon great was the presence of God.

These guys had learned to walk by faith and not by sight. They no longer gave into fear and feelings.

What makes us finish better than we started and what makes our latter greater than our beginning is not that we grow up and become president.

It's not that we become some military hero, or a world-renowned doctor.

It's not that we become wealthy businessmen and women, win the Nobel Peace Prize, or set a world record.

The world would define all these as being successful and most of us would be counted mediocre in comparison.

What makes us successful is do we have the presence of God in our life?

Are we looking through eyes of faith or are we giving into our doubts and fears?

Are we following God when everything around us says that it doesn't make sense?

David says, "Thou wilt show me the path of life..."

Everybody's path is different, everybody's journey is different, and everybody's anointing is different. If God takes you down the path to be a mechanic, find your anointing.

If God takes you down the path to be a construction worker, find your anointing. If God takes you down the path to be a preacher or a teacher, find your anointing.

Whatever path God takes you down, find your anointing and pursue Him with all you have.

There is a Gideon inside all of us.

But it is up to us to get up out of the winepress, accept who God says we are, trust Him and start moving forward.

Chapter 13

One Last Thing

One last thing: You can never pursue your anointing until you first accept Jesus Christ as your personal Lord and Savior. You must repent of your sins.

If you are reading this and you want to make that declaration today, then I invite you to pray the following prayer:

> *Father, I know that I am a sinner and have made mistakes.*
>
> *But I believe that You sent Your Son, Jesus, who is sinless to this earth.*
>
> *I believe that He took my place on the cross and was crucified for me. I believe that on the third day He rose again conquering death, hell, and the grave.*
>
> *I ask You to forgive me of my sins and make Jesus Lord of my life. Thank You, Father, for saving me.*

If you just prayed that prayer and you meant it in your heart, then congratulations! You are a child of God.

Find a good Bible-preaching church, get involved, and begin your pursuit of your own Gideon anointing.

About the Author

Pastor Dustin's journey to ministry was not a conventional one. He didn't surrender his life to the Lord until he was 27 years old. He answered the call to ministry three years later. And then, in 2009, he and Letisha became pastors of Lakeview Community Church (formerly Lakeview Church of God).

As much as Dustin loves pastoring, he feels his greatest calling is to be a husband and a dad.

The Lord has blessed Dustin and Letisha with three wonderful children, Elijah, Emma, and Ethan, who are absolutely the greatest blessings in their lives.

When they are not at the baseball fields, supporting Elijah and Ethan, or taking Emma to horseback riding lessons, they enjoy spending time together outdoors.

Follow Me on Facebook: Dustin Wilds, Author

Made in the USA
Monee, IL
07 October 2021

79137248R00066